I have no degree or qualifications in CV writing. I do, however have experience in finding jobs and getting interviews. I have successfully landed in my desire career. I do possess a Bsc. Degree in Computer Visualization and Games. It's a 3 years undergraduate course. I done in London Metropolitan University.

Why I decided to write this book?

I decided to write this book because just like you I was also unemployed for several years. I know how hard it is to get your desired job. After spending hundreds of hours with employment advisors, I gained a lot of experience in how to write the perfect CV that will ensure an interview date. I learned a lot from my past employment struggles. I eventually landed in a full time job in London.

My success is based on several meetings, hard work and research. I want you to get my knowledge and experience so that you can also find your success in the present job market.

Introduction_____2

How to Write a CV _____6

7 deadly rules to write an award winning C.V.
(curriculum vitae) _____7

CV from the employers point of view _____9

CV/Resume Tips: 3 Ways to Grab Employers Attention 10

How to write a catchy CV_____12

Award Winning CV Exposed! We Reveal the Secret
Behind the Job Winning Resume - Tips to Improve CV_____14

How to Write a CV with Zero Qualifications?_____15

CV From the Employer's Point of View_____17

CV Writing Best Practice - Golden Rules to Make Your CV
Stand Out_____18

Best CV Format - Improve Your Chances to Get an
Interview _____19

Top 3 Mistakes That People Do While Writing Their CV
_____21

Never use CV Templates_____23

Killer Tips on How to Write a Cover Letter That Will
Impress the Employers _____24

Where to find job vacancies? _____26

Speculative Letters _____28

Research will boost your confidence in winning at the
interview _____29

Ways to Prepare For a Job Interview _____31

5 Killer Tips to Impress Employers on Your Interview _32

*Interview Winner Tips*_____*34*

The Secrets to Impress Employers on an Interview ____*36*

Tips and Techniques to Impress Employers on an Interview _____*38*

List of Interview Questions _____*40*

Interviews - Winning Answers _____*42*

Perfect Answers for Interview _____*44*

What to do After an Interview _____*46*

Repeat the process again... _____*47*

*Bonus: 5 CV Examples*_____*48*

How to Write a CV

Writing a CV takes time. It requires patients, experience and knowledge. An eye catching CV will get employers attention. Let me stress out that a CV will not guarantee you a work place, it will however ensure that the employer will invite you for an interview.

In UK there are many employment advisors like the JobCentrePlus, Reed, Seetec, YMCA, etc. I went to all of them! They are very friendly and useful staff. I learned a lot from these establishments.

I was 21 when I first started to look for my first graduate job. I worked in the past (Macdonald's, grocery stores and in family business). So I had some work experience but nothing like a proper graduate work experience.

To land into a market that is full with competition was very tough. But with hard work, persistence and patients I eventually landed into a full time work.

If you are in similar situation, do not discourage it is very much possible to land in to your desired field. I have accomplished and know that millions of others have to. Sure the job market is competitive, taught and saturated but statistics show that no one gets left without a job in their entire lifetime. Eventually people manage to land in to your desired workplace. This is a fact! So do not get discouraged.

M

You're hired! Secrets for CV Writing and Interview Acing Revealed

How to write the perfect CV

Smit Chacha

© Copyrighted 2018

http://www.howwritecv.com/

Introduction

Hi,

My name is Smit Chacha and like you I was also unemployed and looking for work. I struggled a lot in find a job and getting interview. I went to many employment advisors who re-written my CV several times and I also submitted by CVs to several recruitment companies.

7 deadly rules to write an award winning C.V. (curriculum vitae)

C.V. or Curriculum Vitae is the most important piece of document when you are on the job market. With a high quality C.V. you boost drastically your chances to get the job you desire! In this article I will give you 7 deadly rules in how to write an award winning C.V.

The first rule of C.V. writing is to not exceed 2 pages; this gets really hard sometimes especially when you have lots of experience or qualifications.

The second rule is to always start your C.V. with a brief resume. In this area you will write a 2 to 3 paragraph long review about yourself. You will include your very latest qualifications, skills and the types of jobs that you are targeting. You will have briefly explained why these types are very suitable for you (backing up with your skills and qualifications).

The third rule is to list your qualification in a chronological order (very latest first). You will also mention the college name (in capital letters) and address along with the date of accomplishment.
The fourth rule is to list your skills in bullet points.

The fifth rule if to write the most closed match job experience that you had, chronologically (from latest first). You will include the name and address of the employer or company with your position and a sort description of your role. You should also include the month and year of starting and ending dates.

The sixth rule is to write about your interests and hobbies do not skip this rule. The employer knows you only from your C.V. so acknowledging these things helps them to figure out the kind of person you are (socially).

The seventh and the last rule is to reassure the reader that you can provide good references about yourself, by ending the document with "references available upon request".

CV from the employers point of view

Employers normally use your CV as a means to shortlist people for interview and so it is essential that it promotes your best points. Employer is not looking into the spouse's capabilities. Employers often sum up potential candidates by reading the objective. The CV objective needs to demonstrate communication, leadership, future goals, and your ability to move forward in the work environment.

Employers take only a few seconds to decide whether or not you keep your CV, so you have to convince them quickly.

Include an objective up towards the top near where you're going to include all of your contact information. You'll want to also include an academic objective so that it's really clear that you know what you're looking for and you can express that. Include specific skills, such as languages, administrative or computing skills, in a separate section in your CV. Then do not re-list them for every job you've used them in. Include details of each employer, dates of employment and your own job titles. Use concise sentences or bullet points to save space and ensure the document is aesthetically pleasing.

Recruiters reject CVs for any number of reasons, especially if poorly presented or contains basic errors. A poor impression makes recruiters consider wider employability issues as well as things like laziness and fundamental attention to detail, reading and writing skills, etc. Recruitment agencies will ask you for a CV so they can submit it to companies who are looking for your skills. Recruiters will judge your CV on how well you communicate, so choosing the right words, avoiding absolutely all grammar mistakes and spelling errors, etc. It is all about attitude!

CV/Resume Tips: 3 Ways to Grab Employers Attention

Many people ask me this question, which lead me to write this article. I will give 3 killer tips that will grab employers' attention while reading you CV or Resume.

All the tips mentioned in this article are proven to work; this is why people use these techniques to get an interview.

One of the golden rules in writing a CV (curriculum vitae) or resume is to write from employers point of view. So keeping that in mind let's jump to the top 3 ways to grab their attention.

Below are the top 3 ways to grab employers' attention while reading you CV or Resume:

#1 Start your CV/Resume with a short (2/3 paragraph long) profile. In this section you must write a very brief resume of your curriculum vitae, also do not forget to mention the job title you are targeting and your useful skills for that job.

#2 Write your qualifications on the middle of page (especially if you are a graduate). If you are not a graduate then list your skills on the middle of page, because this is the focal point of you CV. Studies have shown that the middle highlighted content grabs attention. So do highlight this section with some bold or background colour.

#3 Never ever exceed 2 pages! This is the most common mistake that people make. Employers are very busy and if they find a very long CV they are likely to ignore it or even throw them away without reading it. So do not exceed 2 pages! Maximize every single page and do not leave any blank space on you CV.

How to write a catchy CV

Everybody asks me "how to I write a catchy CV?" thus I decided to write this article. Here I will provide you useful information, including tips, in how to write a resume from the employer's point of view.

Writing a catchy CV may sound a bit daunting, however as you will see after reading this article that it is not that hard. Once you know what employers want to know when they see you CV everything starts to make sense. And this is what I am going to tell you!

You see, when you apply to a job (this can be via internet or via post) you generally tend you send some kind of details, that will prove that you are suitable for this job. And what are those details? **Your CV of course!**

So you see, the employer knows you only from the CV, therefore you must write a very catchy CV, so that his or she can remember you! From my experience when the employer remembers you means that you are half way there! (Interview is coming soon).

So, how do I write a catchy CV?

- You start you CV with a letterhead where you write your name, address and contact details.
- Below the letterhead you write a very brief review (not more than 3 paragraphs longs) of what your CV is all about. Here you write what sort of work you are targeting, how many years of experience you have on that field and (if applicable) what qualifications do you in that field.

- After the brief review you write your strengths/skills (in bullet points).
- If you are a graduate then just below the skills you write the start and finish date of your course, including the degree name and the University name and address in capital letters.
- After that you write your work experience, start dates and end dates the employers name and address. Also your position and brief descriptions of your duties (no more than 3 paragraphs long).
- We are almost done, after the work experience you write your hobbies and interests <u>(do not skip this)</u> – remember the employers only know you via your CV; this helps the employer to know what sort of person you are. Most people skip this area and as a result they lose their chances of getting an interview.
- Lastly, you finish your letter stating that you are more than happy to provide good references of yourself upon employer's request.

That is it! Simple and catchy CV and this is what employers want! Now that you know it is time to take action, grab these CV templates from this website: and good luck on your job hunt!

Award Winning CV Exposed! We Reveal the Secret Behind the Job Winning Resume - Tips to Improve CV

C.V. or Curriculum Vitae is the most important document for job seekers. This short and simple document evaluates you from the employers prospective. In this article we will reveal the dirty secret behind the Job winning CV.

We will reveal 3 dirty tips that will boost your chances to your dream job!

Tip#1 create a 2/3 paragraph short Overview section on the top of your resume. In this section write 3 things only. They must be very brief and very direct. The things that you need to write in this section are:

1. Your knowledge (education degree as an example)
2. Your ambitions (the position you are applying for)
3. Your skills (your strengths that will impress the employers)

Tip#2 If you have a degree then create a box and write the name of the degree and the date that it was awarded, followed by the Institution name (in capitals). If you do not have relevant qualification, do not worry instead of writing Educational details write your strength, your skills. Write in bullet points and then a 2 paragraph long description of real examples of using these skills.

Tip#3 always write your job experience with the latest date first and then go downward. If you do not have job experience, don't worry you can write your assignment or volunteer work that you have done.

How to Write a CV with Zero Qualifications?

What is a C.V.?

CV is the curriculum vitae which is surely an important document that can land you in a perfect job. If you do not have a good and explicable C.V. then it becomes extremely hard to receive a job as per your wishes and strengths. It becomes most difficult when you do not hold the qualifications and experience in you.

A good C.V. always increases the probability to get the job or an interview. This is the reason that writing up a C.V. is significant.

Two aspects and objectives are important to write a C.V. zero qualification:

It is really important to expose your strengths and to minimize the chances of illustrating your weaknesses like zero qualification. The C.V. should be so impressive and readable that the person taking your interview gets attracted to it in single reading.

Focal Point

It is always claimed that the human eyes are attracted towards the focal point which is natural. The focal point is the one third down section from the top of the document. So try to place all your important things and especially your strengths in this area. As per your thinking write it.

You should always give a second opinion to yourself if the first does not work well.

Presentation

If you are mature in your thinking and you are an objective applicant then it is not at all difficult for you to give a detailed explanation of your career history even if you do not possess a good qualification. Either the C.V. should be one page long or two pages long but never to be one and half a page document because it looks messy.

Thumb rules:

- The C.V. should have more white than the black for an easy reading.
- Create a draft before transferring it into the actual C.V.
- Never ever use the past tense.
- Try to make use of short but sharp sentences that are free from any kind of jargon or waffles.

CV From the Employer's Point of View

Employers normally use your CV as a means to shortlist people for interview and so it is essential that it promotes your best points. Employer is not looking into the spouse's capabilities. Employers often sum up potential candidates by reading the objective. The CV objective needs to demonstrate communication, leadership, future goals, and your ability to move forward in the work environment.

Employers take only a few seconds to decide whether or not you keep your CV, so you have to convince them quickly.

Include an objective up towards the top near where you're going to include all of your contact information. You'll want to also include an academic objective so that it's really clear that you know what you're looking for and you can express that. Include specific skills, such as languages, administrative or computing skills, in a separate section in your CV. Then do not re-list them for every job you've used them in. Include details of each employer, dates of employment and your own job titles. Use concise sentences or bullet points to save space and ensure the document is aesthetically pleasing.

Recruiters reject CVs for any number of reasons, especially if poorly presented or contains basic errors. A poor impression makes recruiters consider wider employability issues as well as things like laziness and fundamental attention to detail, reading and writing skills, etc. Recruitment agencies will ask you for a CV so they can submit it to companies who are looking for your skills. Recruiters will judge your CV on how well you communicate, so choosing the right words, avoiding absolutely all grammar mistakes and spelling errors, etc. It is all about attitude!

CV Writing Best Practice - Golden Rules to Make Your CV Stand Out

Writing a good and effective CV, a CV that stands out from other competitive curriculum vitae takes loads of practice. But with if you follow these golden rules that I will show you on this article you will definitely boost your chances in getting an interview.

Below are the top 3 golden rules that you must follow to stand out your CV from other competitive CVs out there:

- **First golden rule:** always write a profile on your CV. This profile must to exceed 4 paragraphs. In these 4 paragraphs you should write a very brief resume of what your CV is all about (do not forget to state the position you are targeting).
- **Second golden rule:** use the most of the page; never leave a blank page, because a CV should never exceed 2 pages. A large CV is likely to go to the bin. Employers do not have the time to read every single page, so make use the most of your pages and remember do not exceed 2 pages.
- **Third golden rule:** you should always write your education on the middle of the first page (especially if you are a graduate). If you are a graduate this must be your focal point of your CV, so writing on the middle of the first page will make it stand out. Formatting with some graphics is also advisable.

There you go 3 golden rules to stand out your CV from other competitive CVs. Follow these golden rules and you will increase your chances to get an interview.

Best CV Format - Improve Your Chances to Get an Interview

The format in which the CV is structured plays a crucial role in increasing the chances of the applicant to be called for the interview process. There is a great need that the applicant opts for the best CV format in order to match the expectation of the company members.

There are different kinds of the CV which are available each having its own share of merits and demerits. Depending on the current career situation of the applicant there will be one particular format which will best serve the purpose.

For example if a person is choosing to change the company, but wants to remain in the same field, then the chronological structure of the CV will be the best option.

In the other way around in which the person who is changing his field but persisting with the same kind of the job, then the reverse chronological order will be a good option.

There is a type of CV format called the functional CV which will be useful for all the people who are looking to change the direction completely, in this case the format of the CV will be mainly focusing on the achievements, skills and the organizational capability of the person and less importance to the job titles and experience.

There are also targeted and the alternative CV format to help the talented person to apply in the design or other related industries. Hence there should be uncompromised level of the importance be given to the format of the CV. For a particular kind of the job, there will be one format of CV which will be the best.

Top 3 Mistakes That People Do While Writing Their CV

Find why more than fifty percent of the people can't get an interview, as we reveal the top 3 mistakes that people do while writing their CV.

As you know CV or curriculum vitae is the most important document required to get a job. This is why there are so many job agencies that will charge you to write your CV.

And why do they charge you?

They charge you because they are professionals and by being so they know the top 3 mistakes that you are likely to do while writing this important document. And this is what I will reveal on this article.

Below are the 3 things you must avoid doing while you are writing this important document and sending them to employers:

1. Never write on your CV the word "reliable", employers don't like that word instead use words like "hard working", "team leader", etc.
2. Never write the names of companies or colleges in lowercase, names should always start in capital letter.
3. Never exceed 2 pages, employers will not read every page and if they find a CV with more than 2 pages then they are likely to throw them away.

So if you were wondering why you were not getting a positive reply from your CV, probably this is why. And remember to double check your curriculum vitae for possible grammar or spelling errors before sending them to employers.

Tip: Always enclose a covering letter with your CV, employers love this. By doing this extra effort you are giving very positive impression about yourself. It makes employers think that you really want this job.

Never use CV Templates

I know many people use CV templates to build their CVs. I strongly discourage this process. CV templates are easily found online for free but they have been downloaded several hundreds of times that makes your chances in landing for an interview harder.

Think for the employers point of view. Now why would you invite more than 1 person for an interview with similar CVs? It makes no sense!

Create and build your own CV from scratch! This will make it unique and will impress your employers. I suggest that your avoid Ariel font and use Garamond. Never ever use Comic Sans!

Use headers and footers to pin point your keywords. If you submit your CV to online recruiters the use of headers and footer will boost your rankings and views.

For example if your CV is about Web Design, on headers and footer write keywords such as: SEO | Graphic Design | Wordpress | etc.

Make sure that your CV do not exceed more than 1 page. Your employer will not look further. So make full use of your A4 paper.

Font size should not be less than 10 and use grey highlighters to make it more attractive.

If you solely use online recruiters, submit your CV on daily bases. The reason I say that is that it is proven to get more views. People of submit CV will position their CV on the top list for employers. Therefore submitting on daily bases will ensure that you get the most views per day.

Killer Tips on How to Write a Cover Letter That Will Impress the Employers

Writing a cover letter can be a daunting task. But if you follow these instructions that I will show you in this article, writing a cover letter will not only be easy but enjoyable. I will share you with 7 killer tips that will grab the attention to the employers.

So are you ready?

1. Always write a header on the cover letter, the header must have your name in capital letters following by your address and contact details. This information should always be written on the upper right corner of the page.
2. Follow your letter with the employers Name (with initiations abbreviations such as Mr. / Ms. or Mrs.), company name and address.
3. Never ever write your National Insurance number on a covering letter, not even on your CV (curriculum vitae).
4. Always date your letters in this format: "dd/mm/yyyy".
5. Start the body of the letter with the position you are applying for. This is important because the employer may have more than 1 vacancy so they need to know which vacancy you are applying for. Formatting the text in bold is advised.
6. The first paragraph must not exceed 4 lines and in these 4 lines you must describe everything about yourself, this includes your skills, qualifications (if any) and the time span of the experience that you may have that is relevant for the job.
7. Always end the letter thanking the employer and ensuring them that they are free to contact you for more information about yourself.

Tip: Also try not write your birth date on the covering letter, unless the job application states you to write. Writing sensible information like this can lead to identity fraud.

Where to find job vacancies?

You can find job vacancies on online recruiters such as: Reed, Monster, Indeed, Milkround, etc.

Newspapers is also a good place to look for. Online classified ads website such as Gumtree is an awesome place. From my personal experience I can say that Gumtree landed me the most interviews among all the above.

Going to the employers address directly and asking for job vacancies is also advisable. JobcentresPlus and libraries are also useful.

There are ample of opportunities out there, you just need to take an effort to look for. People are being hired on daily bases and job vacancies are always out there. Do not get discouraged you will eventually land in to your desired field and be employed in due time.

Remember one thing people who want to work will work! Job hunting takes time and sometimes people get frustrated. It is normal but I do not remember anyone who never worked in their lifetime.

People eventually get hired in their desired fields. This is a fact!

Ask your neighbors and friends if they know any vacancy out there. It could be local and small but with positive feedbacks you could become an entrepreneurs (self-employed).

I know many professionals who become self-employed and living life at their full potential. Many prefer a full time job and other do both. It is a personal choice.

Self-employed people are need a portfolio and website and a CV. In future they can also join or merge with another company.

Speculative Letters

Nearly 20% of job vacancies get filled with speculative letters. It is an old but still working technique that most youngster avoid them or are not aware off them. Writing a speculative letter is a simple way to introducing yourself to the company without knowing if they have a job vacancy.

Many employers do not have a website. You can still give your details for future reference by sending them a speculative letter.

Employers find hiring and recruiting easier with peoples references.

Sending a speculative letter to the employer will ensure that your details kept in their database, so in future when they start recruiting they can contact you directly.

To get employers details (address and contact name) you can go to Google Maps and type your desired field for example in London "web design companies in London".

Research will boost your confidence in winning at the interview

Once you are invited to an interview, research all you can about the employers. Because they are likely to ask your several questions about their company. If you succeed in answer all their requirements you will win at the interview.

Nowadays it is very easy to find companies details. They are likely to have a website, social media account, Linkedin, etc.

You can also find further details about the company at the company house website (government website). Here you will have details such as board of directors, tax returns, changes in registration, etc.

Knowing all of these will help you to boost your confidence in winning the interview. Find their moto and write a small review about the company and express your intentions in how you can help them in this competitive market.

As long as you express your intentions in how you will become an asset for the company you are in the right track.
Knowing your potential and more importantly expressing them to your employer will definitely boost your chances in winning the interview.

Always think and express your view from the employers point of view. Think like an employer, why they should hire you. This is the key for winning at any interview. Thinking from employers point of view is my method of winning at an interview.

You can practice this at home with a friend or a family member. It is not only fun but productive and helpful.

Ways to Prepare For a Job Interview

Going for an interview is one of the serious events you can ever have in life. This is because; your future is tied to such it. If you succeed, you have a job to earn a living. Hence, you need to study carefully the various ways to prepare for such interviews. Here are some useful tips:

Get ready from home first.

You should begin the preparation from home. Package yourself well through the appropriate dressing code. Use more of black or blue suits with nice polished pair of shoes. Make sure you have a low cut if you are a man and a nice simple hairdo if you are a lady. As a lady; put on flat shoes that will give you balance when you stand before your interviewer. Avoid putting on gorgeous earrings. Just look simple, cute and neat. Above all, be at the venue at least 45 minutes to the commencement of the interview. This will give you ample time to get yourself composed for the interview.

Get prior information about the company

Never go into any interview on presumption. Make sure you have adequate pieces of information about the company and the post you are seeking for. Get information about how their products, their services, their team work modality, their salary scale and so on. This will help you know how to present your answers in a more focused ways.

In all, be ready, confident and stay focused. Be positive and think positive. Do not let any negative thoughts come across you. Follow the above rules and the job is yours!

5 Killer Tips to Impress Employers on Your Interview

Many people ask me for tips about how to empress employers on an interview. So here are 5 killer:

1 - Be there on time.

Punctuality is the sole of business. Getting to the venue on time already gives you 10% score. So, leave your house very early.

2 - Your dressing matters a lot

Here is the best dressing code for your interview

- All clothes must be well ironed
- Solid black or blue suit is the ideal to put on
- Conservative long sleeve shirt or blouse in case of ladies
- Clean and well polished pair of shoes
- Well trimmed low head cut or hairstyle for women
- Well trimmed fingernails

3 - Be the Master over your Nerves

Be in control over yourself. Learn to calm down Always take a deep breathes to gather momentum before you respond.

4 - Be precise in your response

Go straight to the point when you respond to questions. Don't try to show that you know it all. Employers are looking for meekness.

5 - Leave a final impression behind

Make sure there is a particular thing you kept behind for your interviewer especially in your choice of words or response to a particular question asked. Your interviewer will always refer to that whenever you are being discussed.

So there you go 5 killer ways to impress employers on an interview. Just keep up a positive image and be positive, you'll get there!

Interview Winner Tips

In this article I will share with you the best ways to impress employer on an interview

If you want to be the winner in an interview, you have to put the following tips into consideration.

You must start with your appearance. Here is the ideal dressing code for winners:

For the man:

- You must be on your suit preferably black or blue color with a white or blue packet shirt
- Your necktie should be neat with a conservative pattern
- Your shoes should be black and well polished
- Let your haircut be short preferably
- No bears or mustaches. Keep trimmed to the least
- No earrings
- No heavy metals or coins in your pockets

For the ladies:

- Be on your black suit with a jacket and a white top or blouse
- Avoid the over high heeled shoes. Go for a good flat one that can give you freedom to walk
- Long nails are not necessary, but if you must wear them, polish then to look attractive
- You need only one set of moderate earrings
- Avoid heavy perfume, make it lighter.

If you must be a winner, your response to questions asked should be precise. Learn to go straight to the point. Don't digress. Learn to take enough breathe before you answer. When in doubt be polite enough to acknowledge your ignorance of the question asked instead of giving the wrong answer.

In all, you must be a goal getter in all ramifications. Try and leave a good impression behind for your interviewer.

The Secrets to Impress Employers on an Interview

In this article I will share with you the secret in how to impress the employer on an interview.

Below are your wining secrets to impress your employer during an interview:

Make sure you appear very neat and tidy especially with regard to your dressing. This is the first area your interviewer will look at for impression.

How relevant are your answers to the questions asked. Do not go off point. Respond to questions directly with confidence.

Ask your interviewer questions when necessary. Some interviewers will always demand that to discover your level of intelligence quotient.

Maintain a friendly look. Don't be too mean. Lighten the mood of your face and sit up facing the interviewer.

Control your nerves. Don't be tensed up. See the interviewer as a brother or sister you can relate with. One way to achieve this is to take deep breathe each time you feel tensed up. Breathe in enough air and then come down to tackle any posed question.

Know the technicalities of your area of specialization. Being a master in the area you are being interviewed gives you leverage over the rest. Hence, it is necessary for you to do your homework very well.

Make sure there is an impression you leave behind for your interviewer. This makes you to be remembered when the interviewer gets back to the boardroom for discussions with the management on who and who to be chosen.

In all, you must be a positive thinker. Visualize your success before the result comes out.

Tips and Techniques to Impress Employers on an Interview

Below are the best ways to impress your employer during an interview. Follow these tips and succeed on your job prospects!

Your Composure

This begins with your dressing. Make sure you are looking tip top clean. If you are a man, your face should radiate brightness. Don't be too mean.

If you are lady, learn to put on a constant smiling face. This is a great tool to impressing your interviewer especially the male ones. Male interviewers are often time carried away by the way a lady appears. Remember the saying; "first impression matters". You may not get a second chance to correct the first impression. Hence be focused on your mission of getting the job.

Your approach to question asked

Take note of the following:

- Be precise, straight to the point
- Don't digress
- Don't show you know it all, be humble
- Don't rush to answer a question, take a little time to ruminate
- Take deep breathe often and release your responses
- Ask the interviewer necessary questions when due
- Leave an impression behind.

No "Thank You Letter" afterwards

You don't need to write any "thank you" letter to the firm or directly to the interviewer. This may in fact terminate your appointment. It will seem you are coercing the company to employ you. Never try that!

Finally, be on the lookout for the result. Check your email and keep your phone on for the wonderful result you are expecting. Be positive and never give up! Follow the above tips and success is in your way!

List of Interview Questions

Below are a lists of 8 common interview questions that you can always expect to be asked during an interview.

1 - Questions regarding who you are

Here you will be asked to introduce yourself and a little story about your life so far.

2 - Questions about your competence and strengths

Here the employer will like to know your ability to perform given tasks. He may also ask you to throw more light to the position you are seeking for.

3 - Questions concerning team work and bosses

Here your ability to work under instruction is examined. The employer will also try to find out whether you can work within a team.

4 - Questions about your knowledge of the organization

The employer in this segment will like to know how you come to know about their company.

5 - Questions regarding remuneration

Here, you will be asked the salary range you desire per month and how you want it paid.

6 - Ethical questions about stress and work

Here your attitude to work and stress is examined.

7 - Questions regarding your goals and objectives in life

Here, the interviewer will like to know your goal in life and where you are actually heading to. This is necessary, so that they will know which position you may be considered for.

8 - Questions for the interviewer

Here, the interviewer will normally ask whether you have some clarification or other questions for him.

In conclusion. There may be other questions you could be asked to respond. The interviewer holds the key.

Interviews - Winning Answers

In this article I will share with some examples of winning answers you can use to do well in an interview. So are you ready?

Let's use a typical example. Let's say you are a mechanical engineer with specialization in plant repairs and maintenance. Here are some questions you can expect and the tips for your answer:

Question 1: Tell me a little about yourself?

Tip for your answer: When responding to this request focus on both your personal and professional values that link to the job you are applying for. Here is a typical answer you can give:

Answer: I'm an experienced mechanical engineer with extensive knowledge in plant repairs and maintenance. I have done a lot of work for many companies and individuals alike. I like working with people and preferring solutions to different aspects of plant maintenance.

Question 2: Who are you?

Tip for your response: You don't need to begin to tell long stories about your life. What the interviewer wants is a very precise answer about yourself and why you are the best candidate for the job.

Answer: I'm Hilary, from Miami, a former mechanical engineering student of Harvard University. I am an experienced plant engineer who repairs and maintain various generators such as the one you have in your establishment.

In all, you have to employ winning strategy such as these above for answering interview's question. The bottom line is that you have to answer every question with focus to the particular job you are applying for.

Perfect Answers for Interview

In this article I will share a list of perfect answers for your interview questions. So are you ready?

Below are 4 questions examples with possible best suited answers you can give in an interview.

General tips: Answers must link to the job you are applying for. Let's use a typical example. "I am John, from Florida searching for a job in an oil firm"

Question 1: Who are you?

Answer: I'm John Keller from Florida. I'm a mechanical engineering graduate with a flair to engine repairs and services.

Question 2: Why do you want this position?

Answer: I want the position because I want to contribute my quota to the growth of your company, for the good of your every increasing customers out there and for my own earning benefits.

Question 3: How has your education prepared you for this career?

Answer: I studied mechanical engineering in the Oxford University, London with an industrial training experience in Mobil Oil firm for 2 years.

Question 4: What level of Salary do you expect from this job?

Tip for response: Be very precise on this. You must have gathered enough current information on how much the company pay to their former and current staff. With that in mind choose an average amount of what the company pays. For instance, if they are paying $5000 to 10,000, you can make a choice of $7000.

In summary, the above are just sample question with answers. The main point you have to bear in mind is to answer every question by focusing on your area of specialization and on the post you actually want.

What to do After an Interview

You had you interview and hopefully it was a good one. Now you are eager to find out the outcome. To make sure that you get the desired job there are some tips that you should follow. Wait at least 2 days and if you do not get a reply from the employer give him a call or email him.

From my experience emailing first and calling them later on works well in getting interview feedbacks. Every single feedback is important to get and most employers will give tell you where you went wrong and where they were impressed.

If you do not get that job do not get discouraged at least try to get a positive or negative feedback from them. You can ask questions such as:

- "Hi, my name is.... I come for an interview on the .... With .... Just want to get some feedbacks, it's been 2 days and want to know the outcome".

Take their feedback as a positive attitude. The key for success is to learn from your past errors and try to fix them or improve them.

Repeat the process again...

Now you know the secrets for getting a job, how to write a CV/cover letter, how to prepare for an interview and how to ace on the interview. Getting feedbacks and learn from it.

Now the process is same for the next job application....
Congratulations you have graduated in CV writing (on my course)!

Bonus: 5 CV Examples

Smit Chacha

Mobile: 07737345193   DOB: 04/01/1987
E-mail: s_m_i_t@hotmail.com   Portfolio: www.smitchacha.com

Personal Profile

I have a degree in Computer Visualization and Games from London Metropolitan University. During my 3 years course I have learn how to use Autodesk Maya to create 3D models and Cinematic Animations, plus Adobe Photoshop to create and generate UV Texture Maps. I also learn how to program in XNA C# to create Xbox games. I also learn how to use Adobe Flash to create 2D Games and 2D Animations.

Currently I am seeking for full time employment in Games Industry where I can use my 3D Modelling/Animation Skills.

Skills

Platform:

- Adobe Photoshop – Web Mock-up
- Adobe Dreamweaver - Coding
- Adobe Flash – 2D Animation
- Autodesk Maya – 3D Animation
- Adobe After Effects – Video Compositing
- Adobe Premiere – Video Editing

Games Development

- XNA Games Studio
- API
- Autodesk Maya Models
- Collision Detection (Bounding Box Model)
- 3D and 2D Games Development
- Flash 2D Games Development
- Java, C#

Autodesk Maya

- Polygon Modelling
- Nurbs Modelling
- Rigging
- Weight Painting
- Texturing (UV maps)
- Animation / Editing
- Dynamics / Simulation / Visualization

Computer Languages:

- XNA C#
- Action Script 2
- PHP / mySQL
- JavaScript / JQuery
- HTML/xHTML/DHTML
- CSS

Education and Training

London Metropolitan University   Sep 2005 – Jul 2008

Qualifications Achieved: BSc (Hons) Computer Visualization and Games   2:2

Level 1 Modules	<ul><li>Introduction to Programming</li><li>Problem Solving for IT</li><li>Introduction to Computer Graphics</li></ul>	<ul><li>Further Programming</li><li>Introduction to Interactive Authoring</li><li>Time Based Media</li></ul>
Level 2 Modules	<ul><li>Specialist Programming</li><li>Introduction to 3D Animation</li></ul>	<ul><li>Graphics and Imaging</li><li>Data Modelling and Database Design</li><li>E-Commerce Applications</li><li>3D Simulation</li></ul>
Level 3 Modules	<ul><li>Group Publishing Project</li><li>Advanced Development</li><li>3D Character Animation and Effects</li><li>Multimedia Project</li></ul>	<ul><li>Graphics and Imaging 2</li><li>Distributed Game Design</li><li>Prototype Development</li></ul>

Interests & Hobbies

In my spare time I enjoy watching video tutorial and read books about 3D Modelling and Animation, plus I love to browse the web to get more information about games industry such as new technologies and new APIs. I like to be up to date and I am constantly reading blogs and tutorials to get myself busy and up to date.

49

Smit Chacha

Tel: 02082200805
Mob: 07737345195

Email: s_m_i_t@hotmail.com
Portfolio: www.smitchacha.com

About me

I have experience in building blogs and landing pages using Photoshop, Dreamweaver and WordPress. I have done affiliate marketing and managed several E-Commerce websites. Content writing and publishing in English as well as Social Media marketing. List Building and E-mail marketing is what I have done so far.

Education

Sept 2005 - Jul 2008
London Metropolitan University - Bsc in Computer Visualization and Games

Sept 2002 – May 2005
Escola Dr. Antonio Carvalho Figueiredo (Portugal) - Information Technology Diploma (I.T.)

Work Experience

Mar 2010 - Current
Freelancer (Front End Developer/SEO)

- Registering Domain Names and Server FTP
- Installing Content Management System (WordPress)
- Downloading and Installing Various CMS Plug-ins as necessary
- Designing Logos and Graphic Design in Photoshop
- Coding in Adobe Dreamweaver (xHTML, CSS)
- Installing E-commerce Scripts and Data Entry
- SEO - Keyword Research and onsiteSEO(title, meta, alt tags)
- Content Writing/Publishing and Social Media
- Installing and Analysing Web Traffic (Google Analytics)
- Submitting XML sitemap to Google, Yahoo and Bing

Sep 2014 – Feb 2015
Course Coordinator at Harrow International Business School

- Assisting Courses, Printing and scanning documents
- Filing and general administrative duties

Jul 2009 - Feb 2010
Office Administrator at Oxford College of Management Studies

- Printing and scanning documents
- Building forms in Microsoft Word
- Answering phone calls and email correspondence
- Sending parcels and couriers
- Answering student queries and printing student cards

Personal Abilities

- Attention to detail.
- Punctual and reliable.
- Can work without supervision.
- Ability to cope and work under pressure.
- Good written and verbal communication skills
- Able to work as part of a team.
- Having a patient outlook.
- Ability to multitask

Computer Skills

- Microsoft Office
- Adobe Photoshop
- Adobe Dreamweaver
- WordPress
- E-commerce
- SEO
- xHTML / CSS
- Google Analytics
- Google and Bing Webmaster tools

Languages

- English - fluent (read and write)
- Portuguese - fluent (read and write)
- Gujarati - fluent
- Hindi - fluent

Hobbies and Interests

I like reading, watching video tutorials on YouTube, being active on online forums and keeping updated.

I also watch international cricket and IPL

References

Available upon request

Smit Chacha

Web Designer | Web Developer | SEO

Photoshop | xHTML | CSS | JavaScript | JQuery | PHP | MySQL | CMS |

Mob: 07737345195   **Email:** s_m_i_t@hotmail.com   **Portfolio:** http://www.smitchacha.com

Profile

Experience in designing and converting PSD into static xHTML/CSS, can implement JavaScript/JQuery functionality and create complex PHP/MySQL scripts for a full functional dynamic database driven website. Have good analytical skills can easily read graphical/numerical data Google Analytics. Have used several SEO tools and software for keyword research, link analysing, link building, blog commenting, content creation, content distribution, web2.0, social media marketing, email marketing, etc. Experience in running successful PPC campaigns for leads and sales. E-commerce experience and can do multitask when required.

Education

Sept 2005 - Jul 2008
London Metropolitan University - BSc in Computer Visualization and Games

Sept 2002 – May 2005
Escola Dr. Antonio Carvalho Figueiredo (Portugal) - Information Technology Diploma (I.T.)

Skills

- PSD to xHTML/CSS
- HTML5/CSS3
- JavaScript / JQuery
- PHP/MySQL
- CMS
- E-Commerce
- SEO and Link Building
- Google Analytics
- Google AdWords PPC
- Microsoft Office
- Photoshop
- Dreamweaver

Work Experience

Mar 2010 - Current
Freelancer (Front End Developer/SEO)

- Designing Logos, Banners, Posters and Promotional Material for Web and Print
- PSD to xHTML/CSS - Designing Website Wireframe in Adobe Photoshop(PSD) and converting into xHTML5/CSS3 (SaaS and Less)
- Adding/Implementing JavaScript/JQuery functionality.
- Installing Content Management System and various Plug-ins
- Installing E-commerce Scripts and Data Entry
- Registering Domain Names and FTP
- SEO - Keyword Research and onpage SEO(title, meta, alt tags)
- Link Building, Link Wheels and Link Pyramids (offsite SEO) using a variety of software and tools
- Web2.0, Blog Commenting, Bookmarking, Web Scrapping, etc.
- Content Creation and Distribution
- Email Marketing, Social Media Marketing and Video Marketing
- Creating and Managing PPC Campaigns (Google AdWords)
- Installing and Analysing Web Traffic (Google Analytics)
- Submitting XML sitemap to Google, Yahoo and Bing

Languages

- English - fluent (read/write)
- Portuguese - fluent (read/write)
- Gujarati - fluent
- Hindi - fluent

Hobbies and Interests

Cricket, Football and Astrology

References

Available upon request

HTML 5 | CSS3 | JavaScript | JQuery | PHP | MySQL | Google Analytics | Google AdWords | PPC | Email Marketing | Social Media Marketing | Web2.0 | Blog Commenting | Link Building | Content Creation | Content Distribution | Photoshop | Dreamweaver | Front End Developer | Back End Developer | SEO

Smit Mukesh Chacha

Tel: 07737345195
Email: s_m_i_t@hotmail.com
Website: http://www.smitchacha.com

Overview: I have a BSc degree in Computer Visualization and Games from London Metropolitan University and experience in Front End Development, Search Engine Optimization and Google Analytics. Currently I am looking for full time employment in similar fields. My strengths are onsite SEO and offside SEO including: link building, web analytics, keyword research, building cost effective optimized landing pages, A/B Testing and Multi Variable Testing, social media marketing, article marketing and video marketing along with xHTML, CSS, JavaScript/Jquery, PHP, mySQL, Open Source, Dreamweaver and Photoshop.

Key Skills

• Dreamweaver	• xHTML/HTML5	• PHP	• Link Building	• FTP
• Photoshop	• CSS2/CSS3	• mySQL	• Web Analytics	• Open Source
• Autodesk Maya	• JavaScript/Jquery	• SEO	• E-Commerce	

Education

London Metropolitan University   Sep 2005 – Jul 2008
Bsc in Computer Visualization and Games

Escola Dr. Antonio Carvalho Figueiredo (Portugal)   Sep 2002 – May 2005
I.T. Diploma (Technical of Informatics)

Work Experience

Jul 2011 – Ongoing   **Freelance – SEO and Web Analytics**
                                                   Onsite SEO/Link Building/Web Analytics

Key Responsibilities: I have done keyword research, onsite SEO where I targeted the keywords over page titles, meta tags, image alt tags. Done link building using article marketing, article spinning, social media marketing, social bookmarking, video marketing, list building and email marketing. Have tracked the web traffic using Google Analytics and make tweaks based on the web analytical data.

Mar 2010 – May 2011   **Freelance - Front End Development**
                                                   Web Design/Web Development/SEO

Key Responsibilities: I used Adobe Photoshop to create a web template (wireframe layout of the website) the graphics was also optimized for faster rendering. I also created the logo and banners for the website. Then I jump to Dreamweaver where I use xHTML, CSS and JavaScript to build the landing pages. The pages where done with onsite SEO in mind.

Jul 2009 – Feb 2010   **OCMS London**
                                                   Web Design/Web Development/SEO

Key Responsibilities: I used Adobe Photoshop and MS Word to create College prospectus, handbooks, flyers, logo, banners and other promotional material. I also used Dreamweaver code: xHTML, CSS, JavaScript and some PHP/MySQL and built the College website.

Aug 2008 – Jun 2009   **Freelance - Front End Development**
                                                   Web Design/Web Development/SEO

Key Responsibilities: I used Adobe Photoshop to create the web graphics for the design of this website. I also used Adobe Dreamweaver as a web editor and applied CSS styles for the position and typography of the content. The whole website is done using DIV tags and highly SEO optimized. Plus PHP and mySQL for the E-Commerce Website.

| Web Design | Web Development | SEO | Link Building | Web Analytics | E-Mail Marketing | A/B Testing & MVT |
Photoshop | Dreamweaver | xHTML | CSS | JavaScript | Jquery | Open Source | PHP | mySQL

Smit Chacha

Mob: 07737345195
E-Mail: s_m_i_t@hotmail.com

Portfolio:
http://www.smitchacha.com/

Graphic Designer | Web Developer | SEO Specialist | Content Writer | Affiliate Marketer | Forex Trader | Book Writer

Technical Skills

Adobe Photoshop	Microsoft Office	Book Publishing	Webmaster Tools
Adobe Dreamweaver	PSD to HTML5/CSS	Affiliate Marketing	E-Commerce
Autodesk Maya	Content Marketing	Forex Trading	Social Media Marketing
WordPress	SEO	Google Analytics	Link Building

About Me

I have over 10 years experience in building, developing and marketing blogs/websites. Book publishing and distribution, content writing (web and print). Graphic design and marketing. Managing multiple E-commerce stores. Analysing and converting organic traffic into sales. Building and growing social media account followers and likes. Forex trading (fundamentals, technical analysis and risk management).

Education:

Sept 2005 - Jul 2008
London Metropolitan University

BSc in Computer Visualization and Games

Sept 2002 – May 2005
Escola Dr. António Carvalho Figueiredo (Portugal)

Information Technology Diploma (I.T.)

Languages:

English, Portuguese, Gujarati, Hindi - **Spoken**   HTML5, CSS, PHP, MySQL, JavaScript - **Technical**

Work Experience:

Mar 2010 - Current
Freelancer/Web Developer/Affiliate Marketer/Writer/Forex Trader/Employment Advisor

* Registering Domain Names and Server FTP
* Installing Content Management System (WordPress)
* Downloading and Installing Various CMS Plug-ins as necessary
* Designing Logos and Graphic Design in Photoshop
* SEO (Onsite, Offsite)
* Content Writing/Publishing and Social Media
* Installing, Analysing and Optimizing Web Traffic (Google Analytics)
* Book Publishing
* Forex Trading
* CV Writing Service